LE○N

One Pot

NATURALLY FAST RECIPES

By Henry Dimbleby, Kay Plunkett-Hogge & John Vincent

PHOTOGRAPHY BY GEORGIA GLYNN SMITH · DESIGN BY ANITA MANGAN

conran
OCTOPUS

LEON LDN.

ONE POT

LEON

One Pot

NATURALLY FAST RECIPES

FRESH
TODAY

Contents

Introduction

Jack White, lead singer and guitarist of The White Stripes, once posed a thought experiment. Take two singer-songwriters. Give one a studio with a state-of-the-art mixing desk, a professional production team and all the time in the world. Put the other in a room for the weekend with a 4-track tape recorder and a guitar with a broken string. Who do you think will write the better songs?

The answer is of course: the gal with the four-track. Creativity requires constraints. The world is often better stripped back.

This book is for people who want to dial down the complexity of their cooking, but turn the flavour up to eleven. Or indeed those just starting to cook in a flat with a plug-in one-hob oven in the corner of the sitting room. It shows what can be done with just one pot.

You will find something for every occasion here – from a summery chicken casserole with preserved lemons and green olives to a deep, rich, wintery Storecupboard Daube. You have Rigas's Lamb – probably the most cooked of all our recipes – for feeding the hordes, as well as Betty's Quick Prawn Red Curry for a night in front of the telly.

Some dishes in the book, like Jossy's Burmese Spicy Cabbage, are light as you like, whereas others, such as Chicken with 100 Cloves of Garlic, are soft, sweet and deeply savoury.

They are all terrific, and best of all there's no washing up to speak of.

Happy cooking.

Henry & John

FAST ONE-POT SUPPERS

Jossy's Burmese Spicy Cabbage

SERVES 4 (AS A SIDE DISH) • PREPARATION TIME: 15 MINUTES
COOKING TIME: 7 MINUTES • ♥ ✓ WF GF DF

All over Burma you find variations of both cabbage and cauliflower served in this way, with lots of health-giving turmeric and ginger – great on rice or as a side dish.

400g **green cabbage**
2.5cm piece of **fresh ginger**
3 large cloves of **garlic**
1 level teaspoon **turmeric**
juice of ½ a **lemon**
1 tablespoon **fish sauce**
2 tablespoons **peanut oil**
75g roasted **unsalted peanuts**, finely chopped (optional)
a large handful of **fresh coriander leaves**, roughly chopped

1. Slice the cabbage as thinly as you can. Peel the ginger and garlic and slice both into the thinnest possible slivers.

2. Pour 100ml of hot water into a measuring jug, add the turmeric and stir until smooth, then add the lemon juice and fish sauce.

3. Heat the peanut oil in a wok over a medium heat, then add the sliced cabbage and stir for a minute or two, or until it just begins to soften.

4. Now add the slivers of ginger and garlic, and the chopped peanuts, if using, and continue stirring around for another 2–3 minutes.

5. Pour in the turmeric liquid. Stir over the heat for another minute or so, and throw in the coriander leaves just before serving.

TIPS

*   Add another squeeze of lemon juice if you feel it needs an extra lift once you have tasted it.

*   A teaspoon of chilli powder and some sesame seeds also make good additions.

*   It is a good dish to eat on its own with some rice or other vegetables, but would also be nice with some very simple grilled chicken.

John's Wild Mushroom Sauté

SERVES 4 • PREPARATION TIME: 15 MINUTES • COOKING TIME: 15–20 MINUTES • ♥ ✓ WF GF DF V

Genghis Khan was, apparently, so prolific in his 'travels' that most of us are in some way related to him. In that spirit, I have tried here to give you a dish that can provide the grand-daddy from which many variations and related dishes can come – try adding blue cheese, a poached egg, strips of bacon or truffle oil, for example.

6 tablespoons **olive oil** – judge for yourself how much
700g **mushrooms**, sliced – ideally lots of different varieties, but if you only have button mushrooms then that's cool
4 cloves of **garlic**, chopped

some **fresh herbs** you like (such as thyme, tarragon), chopped
a couple of tablespoons finely chopped **fresh parsley**
salt and **freshly ground black pepper**

1. Heat 2 tablespoons of the oil to quite a high temperature (you know, until the steamy effect occurs). Cook the mushrooms until they're just sealed. You'll need to do this in batches: the idea here is to flash-cook the mushrooms and to keep the moisture in, so set each batch aside on a warm plate as you go. And add a little more oil, as needed, for each batch, too.

2. If your mushrooms throw a little moisture into the pan, spoon it out and keep cooking.

3. When all the mushrooms are cooked and set aside, add the herbs to the pan. When the garlic is lightly golden, return the mushrooms to the pan, season with salt and pepper and stir in the parsley.

4. Serve at once.

Quick Bean & Lettuce Stew

SERVES 4 • PREPARATION TIME: 5 MINUTES • COOKING TIME: 15 MINUTES • ♥ ✓ WF GF DF

For days when you have no time, but want something that's properly nourishing.

6 rashers of **bacon**
2 cloves of **garlic**, peeled
4 tablespoons **olive oil**, plus extra for drizzling
¼ teaspoon **fennel seeds**
1 x 400g tin of **chopped tomatoes**
200ml **chicken stock**
1 x 400g tin of **cannellini beans** (235g when drained)
150g **cos lettuce**
sea salt and **freshly ground black pepper**

1. Chop the bacon and garlic. Heat the olive oil in a pan and add the bacon. Cook for a few minutes, then add the chopped garlic and fennel seeds.

2. Pour in the tinned tomatoes and cook on a high heat for 5 minutes.

3. Add the stock and the drained beans, and cook for a further 5 minutes.

4. Season well, add the chopped lettuce and allow it to wilt in the stew before serving.

5. Drizzle with olive oil and sprinkle with lots of black pepper.

TIPS

* This works with all sorts of beans.

* If you want to make it a vegetarian dish, replace the bacon with a few chopped black olives.

Moules Marinières

SERVES 2 • PREPARATION TIME: 25 MINUTES • COOKING TIME: 20 MINUTES • WF GF

If you think 2kg of mussels seems a lot – don't! By the time you have lost the bad ones in the process, then picked them out of the shell, it's a perfect amount. Just serve with a salad and some bread for dunking, or some boiled new potatoes.

2kg **mussels**
50g **butter**
2 tablespoons **olive oil**
2 **banana shallots**, peeled and finely chopped
2 sticks of **celery**, finely chopped
2 cloves of **garlic**, peeled and finely chopped
a large handful of **fresh flat-leaf parsley**, finely chopped
300ml **dry white wine**
salt and **freshly ground black pepper**

1. Wash and scrub the mussels under running water, de-bearding them as you go. The beard is, well, a beard-y thing sticking out the side of the shell. Just rip it off, discarding any mussels that won't close up.

2. Heat the butter and olive oil in a deep saucepan over a medium heat. Add the shallots, celery, garlic and half the parsley and cook for about 5–7 minutes, or until they are soft and fragrant, adding salt and pepper to taste. Be careful with the salt at this stage – the mussels will bring some salt of their own.

3. Once the vegetables are soft and fragrant, add the wine and bring to the boil. Add the mussels and immediately put a lid on. Cook them for about 4–5 minutes, shaking the pot every minute or so. The mussels at the bottom will cook faster than the ones at the top, so make sure you shift them around.

4. Give it all a stir, adding the rest of the parsley. They're done when all the mussels are nicely open. Any that remain closed were dead before you started – so don't even try opening those. Serve immediately.

Pilaff

SERVES 4 • PREPARATION TIME: 5 MINUTES • COOKING TIME: 45 MINUTES • ♥ ✓ WF GF DF

There is possibly nothing more comforting than pilaff – eat it as a side dish or as a simple dinner on its own. This all-in-the-oven version is almost impossibly easy.

4 large **carrots**
2 **onions**
3 tablespoons **olive oil**
400g **short-grain brown** or **white rice**
800ml **chicken** or **vegetable stock**

a large handful of **fresh parsley**
3 **bay leaves**, fresh or dried
juice of ½ a **lemon**
sea salt and **freshly ground black pepper**

1. Preheat the oven to 180°C/350°F/gas mark 4. Peel the carrots and cut them into batons. Peel the onions and slice them into semicircles.

2. Put the carrots and onions into a large ovenproof dish and add the oil, stirring to coat the vegetables. Place in the oven and cook for 20 minutes, making sure the onions don't burn.

3. Meanwhile, measure out the rice, and make your stock. Roughly chop the parsley.

4. Add the rice and bay leaves to the pan of vegetables and cover with the hot stock. The rice should be well covered, but not swimming in too much liquid.

5. Return the pan to the oven and cook for a further 25 minutes, checking regularly to make sure the rice does not cook dry. Add extra stock if it needs it.

6. When the rice is cooked and has absorbed the liquid, it should have a lovely risotto-ish texture. Add the lemon juice and chopped parsley and season well.

TIPS

* Pilaff is always improved by a scattering of toasted flaked almonds over the top.

* You can use other vegetables with this base recipe: sweet potatoes, garlic, peppers...

* Add chicken or slices of leftover lamb to make the dish more substantial.

* If you want to make it more like a risotto, you can use risotto rice. You may need to add up to 200ml extra stock.

Hattie's Pourgouri

SERVES 4 • PREPARATION TIME: 5 MINUTES • COOKING TIME: 20 MINUTES • ♥ DF V

This recipe came to us via Henry's wife, Mima, whose sister Hattie picked it up from her friend Lucy, whose mother used to live in Cyprus. A typically picaresque recipe journey.

2 small **onions** (or 1 large)
3 cloves of **garlic**
a handful of **fresh mint**, **flat-leaf parsley** or **coriander**
3 tablespoons **olive oil**
250g **bulgar wheat**
2 x 400g tins of **chopped tomatoes**
a handful of **almonds**, **pistachios** or **pine nuts**
sea salt and **freshly ground black pepper**

1. Peel the onions and garlic and chop finely. Chop the herbs.

2. Heat the oil in a heavy-based pan. Add the onions and garlic and cook for 5 minutes.

3. Add the bulgar wheat, stir well and add the chopped tomatoes. Stir thoroughly and lower the heat. Put a lid on the pan and cook gently for 15 minutes, stirring regularly, as it can stick easily.

4. When the bulgar is soft, add salt, pepper and the chopped herbs.

5. Toast the nuts in a dry frying pan and scatter them over the top when you are ready to eat.

TIPS

* Drizzle over extra olive oil if necessary.

* Delicious with Greek yoghurt, and brilliant served with roast lamb.

* As good cold as it is hot.

Rachel McCormack's Tortilla Española

SERVES 2–4 • PREPARATION TIME: 15 MINUTES • COOKING TIME: 30 MINUTES • ♥ ✓ WF GF V

This is the basic recipe for a classic Spanish potato omelette. Rachel says the secret of a great tortilla lies in practice and a very good non-stick pan.

125ml **olive oil**
100g **onions**, peeled and finely sliced
375g **potatoes**, peeled and cut
    into small, even pieces

4 **free-range eggs**
a good pinch of **salt**

1. Heat the olive oil in a non-stick omelette pan or small frying pan over a medium–low heat. Add the onions and then add the potatoes to the pan and let them poach in the oil for about 10–15 minutes. Don't let either of them get crunchy; you want them to remain soft.

2. Meanwhile, beat the eggs in a large bowl. Once the potatoes and onions are soft and cooked, strain off the oil into a heat-resistant bowl and set aside. Allow the potatoes and onions to cool a little, then stir them into the beaten eggs and season with salt.

3. Return the pan to a medium–high heat. Add a tablespoon of the potato/onion oil and, when it's hot, pour in the egg mixture. Cook, shaking occasionally to see if the bottom is cooked properly, for about 5–10 minutes. (If the tortilla mix is very thick, turn the heat down a bit to make sure the middle cooks.) Use a palette knife or a saucer to round off the omelette in the pan.

4. Now, if you want to be traditional, Rachel says you should turn the omelette by taking a dinner plate, putting it on top of the frying pan, then flipping it over. Slide the omelette back into the pan, using the palette knife or saucer to make sure it keeps a nice round shape. Cook for about 5 more minutes, then turn out on to a plate.

5. However, if you find that daunting, you could finish the omelette off in the oven, preheated to 180°C/350°F/gas mark 4, for 5–10 minutes. Just make sure you are using a pan with a metal or ovenproof handle. Turn out on to a plate and serve hot or cold with a salad, bread, tomato sauce, mayonnaise…anything you like.

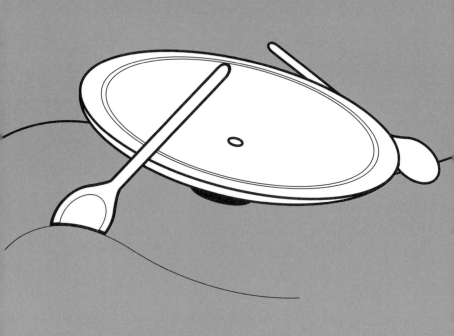

SLOW COOKS, STEWS & CASSEROLES

Storecupboard Daube

Our version of the Provençal classic. As the title suggests, this was born from Kay's storecupboard, the fridge and the little patch of herbs on the roof.

450g **stewing beef**, cubed

1 tablespoon **plain flour** seasoned with **salt** and **pepper**

1 tablespoon **olive oil**

70g **lardons**

1 large **carrot**, peeled and roughly chopped

1 large **onion**, peeled and roughly chopped

4 cloves of **garlic**, peeled and roughly chopped

1 x 55g tin of **anchovies in olive oil**, drained and chopped

4 tablespoons **brandy**

1 bottle of **red wine**

2 big sprigs of **fresh rosemary** or 1 teaspoon **dried rosemary**

a few sprigs of **fresh thyme** or 2 teaspoons **dried thyme**

2 strips of **fresh** or **dried orange peel**

1 x 400g tin of **chopped tomatoes**

55g stoned **black olives**

a small handful of chopped **fresh flat-leaf parsley**, to garnish

salt and **freshly ground black pepper**

1. Heat the oven to 180°C/350°F/gas mark 4. Toss the beef in the flour and shake off the excess to thicken the finished sauce. If you want to use a gluten-free alternative, you can replace the flour with buckwheat.

2. Heat the olive oil in a casserole over a medium heat and brown the meat on all sides.

3. Remove and set aside. (You may have to do this in batches – don't overcrowd the pan, otherwise the meat will turn a nasty grey colour and you won't get the flavour.)

4. Add the lardons, carrot and onion to the oil and cook to soften slightly. After a couple of minutes add the garlic and cook for 2–3 minutes longer. Then scoop everything out and set it all aside with the beef.

5. Add a splash more oil if needed, then add the anchovies, stirring and crushing them into the oil until you get a sort of emulsion. Add the brandy and let it bubble furiously for a couple of minutes, scraping up any residues on the bottom of the casserole with a wooden spoon.

6. Now return the meat, lardons and vegetables to the casserole and add the red wine, rosemary, thyme, orange peel and chopped tomatoes. Season with salt and pepper, and bring the whole lot to the boil. Then put the lid on the casserole and pop it into the oven for about 2 hours.

7. About half an hour before it's due to be ready, open it up and throw in the olives.

8. When it's ready, taste the sauce and adjust the seasoning if necessary. Serve sprinkled with chopped flat-leaf parsley, and accompanied by a bitter leaf salad and some crusty bread or boiled new potatoes.

Chilli Game Hot Pot

SERVES 4–6 • PREPARATION TIME: 15 MINUTES • COOKING TIME: 1 HOUR 15 MINUTES • ✓

This was the product of indecision: chilli or Lancashire hot pot. Our solution – why not combine the two? Feel free to make your own combination of game, or do without the game altogether and make this with lamb or stewing beef.

340g **stewing venison**
340g boned **pheasant breasts**
120g **pigeon breasts**
2 tablespoons **olive oil**
4 cloves of **garlic**, peeled and chopped
1 large **jalapeño chilli**, chopped
125ml **red wine**
1 x 400g tin of **chopped tomatoes**
4 teaspoons **ground cumin**
1 teaspoon **chilli powder** (or to taste)

1 teaspoon **ground cinnamon**
2 teaspoons **dried oregano**
20g **dark chocolate**
2–4 **potatoes**, depending on size, peeled and thinly sliced
a little melted **butter**, to glaze
50g **Cheddar cheese**, grated
salt and **freshly ground black pepper**

1. Heat the oven to 180°C/350°F/gas mark 4.

2. Chop the venison, pheasant breasts and pigeon breasts into small pieces or pulse in the blender. Be careful here: we don't want a mush. Set aside.

3. Heat the oil in a heavy-based casserole and gently cook the garlic and chilli until softened. Add the game and cook until it's browned. Add the red wine and let it all bubble, then add the tinned tomatoes, cumin, chilli powder, cinnamon, oregano, chocolate and salt and pepper. Stir and bring to a simmer. Let it simmer for about 20 minutes, then taste and add more salt and pepper if necessary. Set aside to cool slightly.

4. Layer the potatoes on top of the game chilli in overlapping circles. Brush with a little melted butter and scatter half the grated cheese over the top. Pop into the oven for about 40 minutes, then add the rest of the cheese and cook for a further 5–10 minutes, or until bubbly and golden brown.

5. Serve with some simply cooked or sautéed green vegetables.

Benny's Slow-Cooked Lamb

WITH KOHLRABI & INDIAN SPICES

SERVES 4 • PREPARATION TIME: 20 MINUTES • COOKING TIME: 4 HOURS • ✓ WF GF

Kohlrabi is becoming increasingly available, and is great for slow-cooked dishes because it keeps its shape.

800g **shoulder of lamb**
500g **onions**
1.5kg **kohlrabi** (about 3, medium size)
a 3cm piece of **fresh ginger**
4 tablespoons **rapeseed oil**
200ml **natural yoghurt**

2 tablespoons **medium curry powder**
1 teaspoon **garam masala**
a handful of **toasted flaked almonds**
sea salt and **freshly ground black pepper**

1. Heat the oven to 150°C/300°F/gas mark 2. Cut the lamb into 5cm cubes.

2. Cut the onions into thin rings. Peel and dice the kohlrabi. Peel and finely chop the ginger.

3. Heat the oil in a heavy-based casserole over a medium heat. Add the onions and a sprinkling of salt and cook for 15 minutes, or until caramelized and brown.

4. Add the lamb and ginger. Season and stir. Turn down to a low heat, add the yoghurt and bring to the boil.

5. Add the curry powder and stir for a minute or so. Pour in about 1 litre of water, or enough to cover the lamb comfortably, then add the kohlrabi and bring to a gentle simmer.

6. Cover with a lid, place in the oven and cook for 3 hours, stirring every hour or so.

7. Stir in the garam masala and check the seasoning, then sprinkle the toasted almonds over the curry and serve with basmati rice.

TOP RIGHT: BENNY'S SLOW-COOKED LAMB
TOP LEFT: LEON CHILLI CON CARNE
BOTTOM: CHICKEN WITH GREEN OLIVES

Leon Chilli Con Carne

SERVES 6–8 • PREPARATION TIME: 10 MINUTES • COOKING TIME: 2 HOURS • ✓ WF GF DF

A classic chilli, now a fixture on the Leon menu – a great dish to prepare in advance and freeze (pictured on page 27).

FULL OF SUN

3 **carrots**
2 **onions**
4 cloves of **garlic**
2 sticks of **celery**
3 tablespoons **olive oil**
1kg **minced beef**
3 **bay leaves**
2 teaspoons **ground cumin**
1 teaspoon **oregano**
6 tablespoons **tomato purée**
3 x 400g tins of **chopped tomatoes**
2 teaspoons **smoked sweet paprika**
3 teaspoons **cayenne pepper**
100ml **malt vinegar**
2 x 400g tins of **kidney beans**, drained
sea salt and **freshly ground black pepper**

1. Peel and quarter the carrots and onions and put in a food processor. Peel the garlic and add it along with the celery, then blitz until they are all very finely chopped.

2. Heat the oil in a large saucepan and add the blitzed vegetables. Fry over a gentle heat until the vegetables have softened.

3. Add the minced beef and cook for 10 minutes, or until it is brown all over. Then add the rest of the ingredients and stir well. Cook for 2 hours on the hob, uncovered, stirring now and then. Add a little water if necessary to prevent it from drying out.

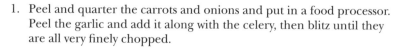

Chicken with Green Olives

& PRESERVED LEMONS

SERVES 4 · PREPARATION TIME: 15 MINUTES · COOKING TIME: 30 MINUTES · ✓ WF GF

A tangy Moroccan dish and a regular summer dish on the Leon menu (pictured on page 27).

1 **onion**
2 tablespoons **extra virgin olive oil**
2 cloves of **garlic**
½ teaspoon **ground ginger**
1 teaspoon **ground cumin**
300g **skinless chicken thighs**, on the bone
500ml **chicken stock**

a strand of **saffron**
1 x 240g tin of **chickpeas**
60g **preserved lemon rinds**
50g pitted **green olives**
a small handful of **fresh coriander**
2 tablespoons **crème fraîche**
sea salt and **freshly ground black pepper**

1. Peel and slice the onion and sauté it for a couple of minutes in the oil in a large saucepan or casserole until just soft. Smash and chop the garlic cloves (don't bother to peel them) and add them to the pan with the ground ginger and cumin. Sauté for a few more minutes.

2. Add the chicken thighs, stock, saffron and chickpeas and simmer gently for 10 minutes.

3. Meanwhile, slice the lemon rind and halve the olives. Add these to the pan and simmer gently for 5 minutes. Roughly chop the coriander.

4. Add the crème fraîche and coriander and turn the heat up slightly for another 5 minutes, to reduce the sauce. Season and serve.

TIPS

* You can use leftover chicken from a roast – just add it towards the end of cooking.

Chicken & Tarragon Casserole

SERVES 4–6 • PREPARATION TIME: 20 MINUTES • COOKING TIME: 1 HOUR 20 MINUTES • ✓

Tarragon is a perfect foil for chicken, adding sweetness and bags of flavour. No wonder it's become such a classic combination. Here, we've used it to add a big herby accent to a one-pot supper. Bundle everything in, pop to the pub or the gym for an hour (or have that walk in the park), then come home to dinner.

6–8 **chicken thighs**, depending on their size
1 tablespoon **olive oil**
1 **onion**, peeled and chopped
1 stick of **celery**, chopped
1 **carrot**, peeled and chopped
1 clove of **garlic**, peeled and crushed
750ml **chicken stock**
1 **bay leaf**
a small bunch of **fresh tarragon** or 1 teaspoon **dried tarragon**

1 **red pepper**, deseeded and cut into squares
1 small **cabbage**, trimmed and cut into quarters through the root
1 tablespoon **crème fraîche**
1 tablespoon **Dijon mustard**
salt and **freshly ground black pepper**

1. Heat the oven to 180°C/350°F/gas mark 4.

2. Trim any excess fat off the chicken thighs. In a heavy-based casserole, heat the olive oil over a medium heat. Brown the chicken thighs in batches on both sides, then remove and set aside.

3. Now turn down the heat and cook the onion, celery and carrot until soft. Add the garlic and cook for a further 2 minutes before adding a dash of the stock. As it bubbles up, scrape up any sticky cooking residues off the bottom of the casserole.

4. Return the chicken to the pan, along with the herbs, red pepper and cabbage. Pour in enough stock to cover the chicken, season with salt and pepper, then put the lid on the casserole and bake in the oven for about an hour.

5. Take the casserole out of the oven and place it on the hob. Remove the chicken, the cabbage and the red peppers to a plate and reduce

the cooking liquor by half, boiling hard for about 3–4 minutes. Then turn down the heat and stir in the crème fraîche and the mustard.

6. Finally, whizz the sauce with a immersion blender for an extra silky finish. Taste and add more salt and pepper if necessary. Return the chicken, cabbage and peppers to the pan to coat them with the sauce and serve at once.

TIPS

* You could serve this with new potatoes or some wide flat noodles.

Giles's Cholent

SERVES 6 · PREPARATION TIME: 20 MINUTES + SOAKING · COOKING TIME: 12 HOURS+ · ✓ WF DF

Henry's friend Giles made this classic Jewish dish a regular weekend feature when his tepid oven only allowed for long slow cooks.

approximately 1.5kg **beef brisket**
2 tablespoons **olive oil**
2 large **onions**
6 cloves of **garlic**
170g **pearl barley**
1 tablespoon **Hungarian paprika**

285g **dried haricot beans** (soaked in water for a few hours)
2 tubs of **fresh beef stock**
sea salt and **freshly ground black pepper**

1. In a medium-sized ovenproof casserole, brown the rolled brisket in olive oil then remove it from the pan and set aside.

2. Peel and slice the onions roughly. Peel the garlic but keep the cloves whole. Put them into the pan and fry until they smell nice.

3. Add the pearl barley and paprika and fry for a minute or two, adding a splash of oil if it all looks stupidly dry.

4. Add the dried haricot beans (soaked for a couple of hours if you remembered). Stir it all about, put the brisket back in and add the beef stock and enough water to cover. Season with salt and pepper.

5. Use a piece of foil under the lid to make a hermetic seal, and place the casserole in the oven at around 80–100°C/200°F/gas mark ¼ (or lower) for around 12 hours. Put it in at around midnight and you'll be spot-on for lunch.

6. Remove the lid at the table and you should find the beans and barley cooked (maybe a bit crunchy at the top if there wasn't enough water, though these bits can be stirred in to lend 'complexity'), and the top third of the brisket poking out like a tiny hippo in a swamp, the fat all yellow and yummy-looking. Application of a fork and spoon should pull the meat apart easily.

Stella Matthews's Cawl

SERVES 8–10 • PREPARATION TIME: 3 HOURS 50 MINUTES • COOKING TIME: 3 HOURS • ✓ WF DF

In Wales, this old recipe is made whenever anybody is coming down with cold or flu symptoms. It banishes them! Or at least lessens them. It's the Welsh echinacea.

600g **beef shin**
2 **onions**, peeled and sliced
1.5 litres **water**
1 small **swede**, peeled and diced
3 **parsnips**, peeled and diced
3 large **carrots**, peeled and diced
3 **leeks**, sliced into rings
4 large **potatoes**, peeled and quartered
a small handful of chopped **fresh parsley** (optional)

1. Put the beef shin and onions into a large saucepan. Pour over 1.5 litres of water, bring it to the boil, then reduce the heat and simmer for about 2 hours, or until the meat is tender.

2. Take off the heat and allow to cool completely. Skim off all the fat from the surface and reserve about 500ml of the resulting beef stock. Shred the meat into small pieces and return it to the empty saucepan.

3. Add the beef stock to the meat. Then add the swede, parsnips, carrots and leeks. You may need to add a little more water to make sure everything's completely covered. Put back on the heat and cook until the vegetables are nearly done – about 15 minutes, then add the potatoes and cook until they're soft.

4. Serve in bowls, sprinkled with the chopped parsley, with crusty bread and strong Cheddar cheese.

TIPS

* You can buy shin of beef either cubed or in slices on or off the bone. If it's on the bone, make sure you use the marrow!

Rigas's Lamb

SERVES 6–8 • PREPARATION TIME: 20 MINUTES • COOKING TIME: 3 HOURS 30 MINUTES • DF

This dish was made for us by our (Greek) friend Dimitri, from a recipe that has been handed down in his family for generations.

1 **leg of lamb**, on the bone
5 cloves of **garlic**, peeled
a small bunch of **fresh mint**
2 **onions**, peeled
2 x 400g tins of **chopped tomatoes**
75ml **extra virgin olive oil**

300g **risoni**, **kritharaki** or **small macaroni**
2 tablespoons **dried mint**
sea salt and **freshly ground black pepper**

1. Heat the oven to 150°C/300°F/gas mark 2.

2. With the tip of a sharp knife, make 6 or 7 quite deep holes on both sides of the meat. Stuff these with small pieces of garlic, followed by an equal amount of salt and pepper mixed together. Plug the holes with a couple of leaves of fresh mint, and season the meat with a little more salt and pepper.

3. Finely chop the onions and put them into a large roasting dish. Add the tomatoes and oil and stir well. Put the meat on top, and place in the oven.

4. Cook for 3½ hours. Keep adding water to the sauce to prevent it from drying out. If you like, you can baste the lamb with spoonfuls of the sauce so that it forms a crust of caramelized onions on the meat.

5. When 20 minutes of cooking time is left, add a cup of water to the sauce and stir in the risoni or macaroni.

6. Season, sprinkle well with dried mint (use more than you think you should – it adds a peppery kick to the sauce) and put back into the oven until the pasta is tender. The risoni will expand and absorb the liquid sauce, which in turn will have absorbed all the juices from the meat. Keep adding water and stirring every 5–10 minutes if you need to so that the pasta stays moist and doesn't stick.

TIPS

* To serve, try green beans, allowed to cool slightly and sprinkled with lemon juice, olive oil and salt and pepper. Otherwise a green salad makes a good accompaniment.

CURRIES

Dalston Sweet Potato Curry

SERVES 6 • PREPARATION TIME: 15 MINUTES • COOKING TIME: 40 MINUTES • ✓ WF GF DF V

A sweet, rich, everyday vegetable curry.

1 **onion**
1 tablespoon **sunflower oil**
4 cloves of **garlic**
a 2.5cm piece of **fresh ginger**
2 teaspoons **ground coriander**
2 teaspoons **ground cumin**
½–1 teaspoon **cayenne pepper**,
    depending how hot you like it
1 level teaspoon **turmeric**

1 x 400g tin of **chopped tomatoes**
4 **sweet potatoes** (not giant ones),
    peeled and cubed
1 **cauliflower**
1 x 400g tin of **coconut milk**
100g **cashew nuts**
sea salt and **freshly ground
    black pepper**

1. Peel the onion, roughly chop and fry gently in the oil in a large saucepan for 5 minutes. Peel and grate the garlic and ginger, add to the pan and fry for 1 minute. Add the spices and cook for a further 2 minutes until they are fragrant.

2. Add the tomatoes and sweet potatoes. Cook for about 30 minutes, adding water if it seems to be drying out.

3. Divide the cauliflower into florets and add them to the pan with the coconut milk.

4. Put the lid on and simmer for around 8 minutes, or until soft.

5. Meanwhile, gently toast the cashew nuts in a dry frying pan.

6. Season to taste and add the nuts just before serving.

TIPS

* Add spinach, coriander or peas for a bit of colour.
* Serve with rice and a blob of natural yoghurt.

TOP: DALSTON SWEET POTATO CURRY
BOTTOM LEFT: JOSSY'S CHICKEN LIVER CURRY
BOTTOM RIGHT: COCONUT CHICKEN & PETITS POIS CURRY

Jossy's Chicken Liver Curry

SERVES 4–6 • PREPARATION TIME: 20 MINUTES • COOKING TIME: 35 MINUTES • ✓ WF GF

One for the liver lovers – tangy and meaty and very cheap (pictured on page 39).

800g **chicken livers**
3 tablespoons **natural yoghurt**
2 medium **onions**
3 cloves of **garlic**
a 2.5cm piece of **fresh ginger**
2 tablespoons **tikka paste**
3 tablespoons **lemon juice**
25g **butter**
1 teaspoon **cumin seeds**
1 x 400g tin of **chopped tomatoes**
a large handful of **fresh coriander leaves**
sea salt and **freshly ground black pepper**

1. Cut the chicken livers into 2.5cm pieces (removing any sinewy bits), place in a bowl, add the yoghurt and set aside.

2. Peel the onions, garlic and ginger and roughly chop. Put one of the onions into a blender with the garlic, ginger, tikka paste and lemon juice and whizz to a paste.

3. Tip the mixture into a casserole, place over a low heat and simmer gently for about 15 minutes, stirring frequently.

4. Finely slice the remaining onion and add to the pan with the butter, cumin seeds, chicken livers and tomatoes. Simmer for a further 15 minutes, stirring occasionally.

5. Season with roughly chopped coriander and salt and pepper to taste.

TIPS

* Best served with basmati rice and a salad.

Coconut Chicken & Petits Pois Curry

SERVES 4–6 • PREPARATION TIME: 10 MINUTES • COOKING TIME: 15 MINUTES • ✓ WF GF

A fantastically quick curry to make (pictured on page 39).

6 boneless and skinless **chicken breasts**
25g **butter**
2 teaspoons **nigella seeds** (black onion seeds)
2 tablespoons **tikka paste**
300ml **coconut milk**
200g **frozen peas**
a handful of **fresh coriander leaves**
sea salt and **freshly ground black pepper**

1. Slice the chicken breasts into thin strips.

2. Melt the butter in a heavy-based frying pan. Add the chicken and nigella seeds and cook for between 8–10 minutes, or until the chicken is cooked through.

3. Stir in the tikka paste, coconut milk and peas. Bring gently to the boil, stirring all the time, and simmer for a minute or two.

4. Chop the coriander, add to the pan and season to taste.

TIPS

* All the ingredients for this lightning recipe can be kept in your freezer or storecupboard, so grab the chicken breasts on your way home and you can be eating a delicious creamy curry within minutes.

* Basmati rice, which takes 10 minutes to cook, completes the meal.

Betty's Quick Prawn Red Curry

SERVES 2 • PREPARATION TIME: 10–15 MINUTES • COOKING TIME: 10 MINUTES • ✓ WF GF DF

Here's a quick trip to Thailand in one very simple curry.

1 tablespoon **vegetable oil**
2 cloves of **garlic**, peeled and finely chopped
1 tablespoon **Thai red curry paste**
200ml **coconut milk**
2 teaspoons **granulated sugar**
2 teaspoons **nam pla** (fish sauce)
a 2cm square of **fresh ginger**, peeled and slivered

12 **fresh basil leaves**, plus a few to garnish
3 **kaffir lime leaves**, slivered
1 tablespoon **roasted unsalted peanuts**, crushed
300g **large prawns or prawn tails**
a squeeze of **lime juice**
1 large **red chilli**, finely slivered

1. In a wok or a pan, heat the oil and fry the garlic until it just begins to brown. Add the curry paste and stir in well, until you can really smell it.

2. Add 100ml of the coconut milk and bring to the boil. Add 100ml of water and bring back to the boil, then add the rest of the coconut milk and bring to the boil again. Add the sugar and nam pla and stir in well.

3. Add the ginger, basil, 2 of the lime leaves and the peanuts, one ingredient at a time, stirring well after each addition. Then stir in the prawns. They will turn pink when they are cooked through – in no more than a minute or two.

4. Add a squeeze of lime, then turn out into a serving dish. Garnish with the slivered chilli, the last lime leaf and a few leaves of basil. Serve with jasmine rice.

TIPS

* When you buy your curry paste, make sure you get a good one. Kay recommends the Mae Ploy brand.

* Remember that chillies freeze really well, so don't worry if you have to buy a whole pack. Just freeze them for next time. The same goes for lime leaves – pop them into a plastic bag and freeze them too, and coconut milk: freeze it in an ice cube tray.

John's Thai Curry

SERVES 4 • PREPARATION TIME: 15 MINUTES • COOKING TIME: 15 MINUTES • ✓ WF GF DF

The green chicken curry has become the chicken tikka masala of the western Thai restaurant scene. You can replicate it in your own home very easily and quickly, thanks to the Thai curry pastes available. However, be sure to steer well clear of ready-made sauces: they will leave you disappointed. Use only a high quality paste and start from there.

4 **chicken thighs**
1 tablespoon **olive oil**
2–3 tablespoons **Thai curry paste**
1 x 400ml tin of **coconut milk**
1 x 225g tin of **bamboo shoots**
100g **Thai aubergines**

2 tablespoons **Thai fish sauce**
a few leaves of **fresh Thai sweet basil**
sea salt and **freshly ground black pepper**

1. Remove the meat from the chicken thighs and cut into thin strips.

2. Heat the olive oil in a large frying pan, add the Thai curry paste, and stir the paste into the oil as you fry on a hot heat for a minute.

3. Gradually add the coconut milk, followed by the chicken.

4. Drain and add the bamboo shoots and the Thai aubergines, and simmer for 10 minutes.

5. Add the fish sauce, then taste and adjust the seasoning with salt and pepper if you want to.

6. Sprinkle the curry with sweet basil and serve with rice.

TIPS

* If you cannot find Thai sweet basil, use normal basil instead.

* Get the right paste (I recommend Mae Ploy), and don't buy the sauces that come in jars.

* The chicken will cook more quickly and taste much better if it is cut into thin strips rather than big chunks.

* Add the coconut milk slowly, and stir as you do so to avoid the paste and the coconut milk separating.

* Thai aubergines are nothing like the aubergines we are used to. You can buy them in larger supermarkets or Thai shops in jars. If you cannot find them, you can add peas instead.

Mum's Chicken Curry

(MURG KORMA)

SERVES 4 • PREPARATION TIME: 20 MINUTES •
COOKING TIME: 40 MINUTES • ♥ ✓ WF GF DF

Our friend Mamta Gupta makes many different curries. This is the one her daughters request most often. It's always known at their house as Mum's Chicken Curry.

2 tablespoons **vegetable oil**
½ teaspoon **cumin seeds**
1 large **onion**, peeled and chopped – about 250g
a 2cm piece of **fresh ginger**, peeled and chopped
2–3 cloves of **garlic**, peeled and chopped
2–3 **tomatoes**, chopped, or 2–3 tablespoons **tomato purée**
2 tablespoons **dried fenugreek** or **methi leaves** (optional)
500g **chicken thighs** on the bone
½ teaspoon **garam masala**
a handful of **fresh coriander leaves**, chopped, to garnish
salt

The whole spices (see tip opposite):
1 **bay leaf**
1–2 pieces of **cinnamon stick** or **cassia bark**
2 large **cardamom pods**
3–4 small **green cardamom pods**
5–6 **black peppercorns**
4–5 **cloves**

The ground spices:
1 teaspoon **ground turmeric**
2 teaspoons **ground coriander**
1 teaspoon **paprika** (optional)
½ teaspoon **chilli powder**, or to taste

1. Heat the oil in a heavy-based wok or sauté pan, and add the cumin seeds and the whole spices. Cook until the cumin seeds begin to sputter, being careful not to let them burn. Add the onion, ginger and garlic, and fry until browned and almost caramelized, stirring frequently so nothing sticks. Now stir in the ground spices, and cook for a few seconds to bring out their flavour.

2. Add the tomato and the fenugreek or methi leaves, if using, and cook, stirring frequently, until the oil separates. Finally, add the skinned chicken thighs, and cook over a medium–high heat, stirring frequently, until the chicken is well coated and sealed.

MAMTA WITH KAVITA, 1972

3. Cover the pan, and cook over a low–medium heat for about 15–20 minutes, or until tender. When the chicken is cooked, if the sauce looks a little thick, add some water. Turn off the heat and stir in the garam masala and half of the coriander. Season with salt, to taste.

4. Garnish with the remaining coriander and serve with rice, naan, roti or chapati.

TIPS

* If you are short of one or more of the whole spices, leave them ALL out; use with 1½ teaspoons of garam masala instead.

Garam Masala

MAKES 50G • PREPARATION TIME: 2–5 MINUTES • COOKING TIME: NONE • ♥ ✓ WF GF DF V

Garam means hot, and masala means spice mix. Since many store-bought versions are padded out with extra cumin or coriander, Mamta suggests you make your own for that proper punch.

1 tablespoon **black peppercorns**
1 teaspoon **cloves**
4–5 **brown cardamom pods**
4–5 **dried bay leaves**
a 6cm piece of **cinnamon stick** or **cassia bark**
4–5 **green cardamom pods** (optional)
½ a **nutmeg**, freshly grated (optional)
1–2 tablespoons **cumin seeds** (optional)

1. Grind all the ingredients together finely in an electric coffee grinder or in a pestle and mortar. Then sieve to remove any husks or fibres.

2. Store in an airtight container.

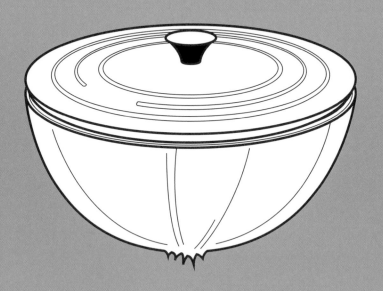

POT
ROASTS

Chicken Pot Roast

SERVES 4 · PREPARATION TIME: 15 MINUTES · COOKING TIME: 1½–2 HOURS · WF GF DF

This is the classic simple supper – pop it all into a large pot when you get home and spend your evening doing something you enjoy.

5 rashers of **bacon**
500g **carrots**
500g **potatoes**
3 **onions**
1 whole bulb of **garlic**
6 sprigs of **fresh thyme**
2 tablespoons **extra virgin olive oil**

300ml **white wine**
1 **whole chicken**, 1.5–2kg in
weight
sea salt and **freshly ground
black pepper**

1. Heat the oven to 190°C/375°F/gas mark 5.

2. Roughly chop the bacon. Peel the carrots, but leave the potatoes and onions unpeeled. Roughly chop the carrots and potatoes, and cut the onions into quarters. Cut the unpeeled garlic bulb in half across the middle. Place all these into a casserole with the thyme and seasoning. Add 1 tablespoon of the olive oil and toss thoroughly. Pour in the white wine.

3. Rub the chicken with the remaining tablespoon of olive oil and season well. Place on top of the vegetables.

4. Cook for 1 hour, covered, then remove the lid and cook for another 30 minutes to 1 hour to brown the chicken and, depending on its size, ensure it is cooked through.

TIPS

* This is a very versatile dish. Almost any mix of vegetables, herbs and spices will work as the base. Try thinking in themes: winter pot roast – using root veg and sage; German pot roast – using cabbage, some pieces of sausage and juniper.

* You don't need to stick to chicken. You can use this method with almost any meat – game, beef (particularly the cheap cuts) or lamb. For tougher meats you may need to use more liquid and cook for longer.

* If you don't use potatoes, this goes very well with tagliatelle. The combination of the juice and simple buttered pasta is one of life's great pleasures.

Winter Vegetable Herb Pot Roast

SERVES 4–6 • PREPARATION TIME: 15 MINUTES •
COOKING TIME: 1 HOUR 30 MINUTES • ♥ ✓ WF GF DF V

A great way to use up ungainly winter vegetables. The trick is the flash of raw garlic and parsley at the end, which lifts everything.

For the pot
2 **onions**
4 **parsnips**
1 **butternut squash**
3 **carrots**
a large handful of **fresh sage**
2 tablespoons **extra virgin olive oil**
1 glass of **white wine**
1 x 400g tin of **flageolet beans**
sea salt and **freshly ground black pepper**

To finish
3 cloves of **garlic**
a handful of **fresh flat-leaf parsley**
a dash of **olive oil**

1. Heat the oven to 200°C/400°F/gas mark 6.

2. Peel and slice the onions. Peel the parsnips and quarter them lengthways. Deseed the butternut squash and cut it into large chunks (leaving the skin on). Peel the carrots and slice them diagonally. Roughly chop the sage.

3. Put all the vegetables, except the beans, into a casserole with the olive oil, wine and sage. Cook in the oven for 1 hour with the lid on.

4. Add the drained beans and cook for another 30 minutes with the lid off. You may want to add a little water if it gets too dry.

5. Just before serving, blitz the garlic with the parsley and a little olive oil. Season and stir into the casserole.

TIPS

* You can use any combination of winter vegetables – celeriac, pumpkin, potatoes, shallots, celery, turnips, swede, beetroot, all work well.

* Don't be afraid to mix in a few greens – kale, cabbage, winter and spring greens will all be happy in the pot.

* Try popping in a few chestnuts.

Spanish Pot Roast

SERVES 4 • PREPARATION TIME: 15 MINUTES • COOKING TIME: 1½–2 HOURS • ♥ ✓ WF GF DF

Warm and spicy.

3 **onions**
3 **carrots**, peeled
1 whole bulb of **garlic**
4 **tomatoes**
3 teaspoons **fennel seeds**
2 tablespoons **olive oil**
2 heaped teaspoons **smoked
  sweet paprika**

1 **whole chicken**, 1.5–2kg
  in weight
2 tablespoons **sherry vinegar**
250ml **white wine**
sea salt and **freshly ground
  black pepper**

1. Heat the oven to 190°C/375°F/gas mark 5.

2. Quarter the onions (no need to peel them). Cut the carrots into long batons. Slice the bulb of garlic across and quarter the tomatoes.

3. Put all the vegetables in the bottom of a large casserole with the fennel seeds, 1 tablespoon of the olive oil and 1 teaspoon of the paprika. Season well and stir.

4. Rub the remaining oil and paprika into the chicken along with some salt and pepper. Place the chicken on top of the vegetables and pour in the vinegar and white wine.

5. Cook in the oven for 1 hour, covered, then remove the lid and cook for another 30 minutes to 1 hour to brown the chicken and, depending on its size, ensure it is cooked through.

TIPS

* Add some peeled potato chunks to the pot for a full meal in one pot.
* Otherwise serve with rice or pasta.
* If you like a bit of spice use hot paprika in place of the sweet stuff.
* Great with some added chunks of chorizo mixed in with the vegetables.

TOP: SPANISH POT ROAST
BOTTOM RIGHT: INDIAN POT ROAST CHICKEN
BOTTOM LEFT: PORK BELLY WITH TURNIPS & PRUNES

Indian Pot Roast Chicken

SERVES 4–6 • PREPARATION TIME: 15 MINUTES • COOKING TIME: 1½–2 HOURS • WF GF

The potatoes in this dish pick up a wonderful lemony, curried flavour (pictured on page 55).

3 cloves of **garlic**
4 tablespoons **natural yoghurt**
2 teaspoons **turmeric**
2 teaspoons **ground cinnamon**
2 teaspoons **ground coriander**
1 teaspoon **chilli powder**
750g **Charlotte potatoes** or
   new potatoes

1 teaspoon **vegetable oil**
1 **lemon**
1 **whole chicken**, 1.5–2kg
   in weight
a handful of **fresh coriander
   leaves**
sea salt and **freshly ground
   black pepper**

1. Heat the oven to 190°C/375°F/gas mark 5.

2. Peel and grate the garlic into a bowl, add the yoghurt, spices and chilli and mix well.

3. Slice the unpeeled potatoes fairly thinly and place in a large casserole dish with the oil. Halve the lemon and slice one half finely. Add the lemon slices to the potatoes. Season with salt and pepper.

4. Smear the yoghurt mixture all over the chicken and place it on top of the potatoes. Put the other half of the lemon inside the cavity of the bird.

5. Cook, covered, in the oven for 1 hour, then remove the lid and cook for another 30 minutes to 1 hour to brown the chicken and, depending on its size, ensure it is cooked through.

6. Remove the chicken from the casserole and place on a board. Put the potatoes into a serving dish and sprinkle with the coriander leaves.

TIPS

* If you don't have the spices you could use a curry paste or powder in their place.

* Also good is to replace the spices with a tablespoon of lime pickle blended finely with the yoghurt.

* To allow the yoghurt and spice mixture to permeate the chicken more, pull the skin away from the breast gently and spread some of the yoghurt underneath the skin.

* Serve with a salad or simple green vegetables.

Pork Belly with Turnips & Prunes

SERVES 4 • PREPARATION TIME: 10 MINUTES • COOKING TIME: 3 HOURS • ✓ WF GF DF

This dish is so simple to make and so full of flavour (pictured on page 55).

a chunk of **pork belly** that fits into your casserole,
    about 1–1.5kg in weight
2 tablespoons **olive oil**
1 **turnip**
2 large **carrots**
1 large **onion**
100g **pitted prunes**
4 **star anise**
15 **coriander seeds**
1 bottle of **white wine** (it's worth it)
sea salt and **freshly ground black pepper**

1. Heat the oven to 180°C/350°F/gas mark 4.

2. Season the skin of the pork well, then brown it in the olive oil in a casserole. Remove the pork and set aside.

3. Peel the turnip and slice into 5mm rounds. Peel the carrots and cut into batons. Peel and roughly chop the onion. Halve the prunes. Add all the vegetables to the casserole with the prunes and spices.

4. Add the wine, then return the pork to the casserole and put the lid on.

5. Cook for 2½ hours (at least), until the meat is very tender – basting every 30 minutes and adding water if the vegetables dry out too much.

6. Remove the lid and cook for a further 30 minutes before serving.

TIPS

* The vegetables should end up as a glossy thick mixture at the end of cooking.

* You can carefully cut the skin off the pork and roast it in the oven for 15 minutes at 200°C/400°F/gas mark 6 to crisp it up, while the pork stays in the casserole.

* If you think the wine is a bit extravagant, you can always replace most of it with chicken stock.

Chicken with 100 Cloves of Garlic

SERVES 6 · PREPARATION TIME: 10 MINUTES · COOKING TIME: 1 HOUR 30 MINUTES · ♥ ✓ WF GF DF

A pot-roast to show off with, and so simple; the garlic warms and softens and sweetens and creates a lovely depth of flavour.

1 medium-sized **whole chicken**, 1–1.5kg in weight
a glug of **extra virgin olive oil**
100 cloves of **garlic** (about 12 bulbs)
3 large handfuls of **fresh thyme**
200ml **red wine vinegar**
sea salt and **freshly ground black pepper**

1. Heat the oven to 180°C/350°F/gas mark 4.

2. Smear the chicken with olive oil and plenty of salt and pepper. Break up the garlic bulbs into cloves, but do not peel them.

3. Stuff the chicken with the thyme and about 20 cloves of garlic. Place the rest of the garlic in a casserole and nestle the chicken on top. Pour in the vinegar.

4. Cover and cook for approximately 1 hour, adding up to 200ml of water if necessary to stop it drying out.

5. Remove the lid and cook for a further 30 minutes until the chicken is browned.

TIPS

* Serve with tagliatelle and a green salad with balsamic dressing.

* Try squeezing the roasted garlic from its skin and spread it on bread with a little salt: a delicious way to use up the garlic which will be left over.

CONVERSION CHART FOR COMMON MEASURES

LIQUIDS

15 ml	½ fl oz
25 ml	1 fl oz
50 ml	2 fl oz
75 ml	3 fl oz
100 ml	3½ fl oz
125 ml	4 fl oz
150 ml	¼ pint
175 ml	6 fl oz
200 ml	7 fl oz
250 ml	8 fl oz
275 ml	9 fl oz
300 ml	½ pint
325 ml	11 fl oz
350 ml	12 fl oz
375 ml	13 fl oz
400 ml	14 fl oz
450 ml	¾ pint
475 ml	16 fl oz
500 ml	17 fl oz
575 ml	18 fl oz
600 ml	1 pint
750 ml	1¼ pints
900 ml	1½ pints
1 litre	1¾ pints
1.2 litres	2 pints
1.5 litres	2½ pints
1.8 litres	3 pints
2 litres	3½ pints
2.5 litres	4 pints
3.6 litres	6 pints

WEIGHTS

5 g	¼ oz
15 g	½ oz
20 g	¾ oz
25 g	1 oz
50 g	2 oz
75 g	3 oz
125 g	4 oz
150 g	5 oz
175 g	6 oz
200 g	7 oz
250 g	8 oz
275 g	9 oz
300 g	10 oz
325 g	11 oz
375 g	12 oz
400 g	13 oz
425 g	14 oz
475 g	15 oz
500 g	1 lb
625 g	1¼ lb
750 g	1½ lb
875 g	1¾ lb
1 kg	2 lb
1.25 kg	2½ lb
1.5 kg	3 lb
1.75 kg	3½ lb
2 kg	4 lb

OVEN TEMPERATURES

110°C	(225°F)	Gas Mark ¼
120°C	(250°F)	Gas Mark ½
140°C	(275°F)	Gas Mark 1
150°C	(300°F)	Gas Mark 2
160°C	(325°F)	Gas Mark 3
180°C	(350°F)	Gas Mark 4
190°C	(375°F)	Gas Mark 5
200°C	(400°F)	Gas Mark 6
220°C	(425°F)	Gas Mark 7
230°C	(450°F)	Gas Mark 8

MEASUREMENTS

5 mm	¼ inch
1 cm	½ inch
1.5 cm	¾ inch
2.5 cm	1 inch
5 cm	2 inches
7 cm	3 inches
10 cm	4 inches
12 cm	5 inches
15 cm	6 inches
18 cm	7 inches
20 cm	8 inches
23 cm	9 inches
25 cm	10 inches
28 cm	11 inches
30 cm	12 inches
33 cm	13 inches

Working with different types of oven

All the recipes in this book have been tested in an oven without a fan. If you are using a fan-assisted oven, lower the temperature given in the recipe by 20°C. Modern fan-assisted ovens are very efficient at circulating heat evenly around the oven, so there's also no need to worry about positioning.

Regardless of what type of oven you use you will find that it has its idiosyncrasies, so don't stick slavishly to any baking recipes. Make sure you understand how your oven behaves and adjust accordingly.

Key to Symbols/Nutritional Info

♥	LOW SATURATED FATS
✓	LOW GLYCAEMIC (GI) LOAD
WF	WHEAT FREE
GF	GLUTEN FREE
DF	DAIRY FREE
V	VEGETARIAN
TIPS	COOKING TIPS, EXTRA INFORMATION AND ALTERNATIVE IDEAS.

Index

An Hachette UK Company
www.hachette.co.uk

First published in Great Britain in 2014
by Conran Octopus Limited, a division of
Octopus Publishing Group, Carmelite House,
50 Victoria Embankment, London EC4Y 0DZ
www.octopusbooks.co.uk

This book includes a selection of previously
published recipes taken from the following titles:
Leon Naturally Fast Food and *Leon Family & Friends*.

Publisher: Alison Starling
Senior Editor: Sybella Stephens
Assistant Editor: Meri Pentikäinen
Art Director: Jonathan Christie
Art Direction, Design and Illustrations:
   Anita Mangan
Additional illustrations: Ella MacLean
Design Assistant: Abigail Read
Photography: Georgia Glynn Smith
Production Manager: Katherine Hockley

ISBN 978 1 84091 670 6

Printed and bound in China

10 9 8 7 6 5

A note from the authors…
Medium eggs should be used unless
otherwise stated.
We have endeavoured to be as accurate as
possible in all the preparation and cooking
times listed in the recipes in this book.
However, they are an estimate based on
our own timings during recipe testing, and
should be taken as a guide only, not as the
literal truth. We have also tried to source
all our food facts carefully, but we are not
scientists. So our food facts and nutrition
advice are not absolute. If you feel you
require consultation with a nutritionist,
consult your GP for a recommendation.

Also available in the Little Leon series...

Breakfast & Brunch • Smoothies, Juices & Cocktails
Soups, Salads & Snacks • Brownies, Bars & Muffins • Fast Suppers